Presented to:

_____

Presented by:

_____

Date:

_____

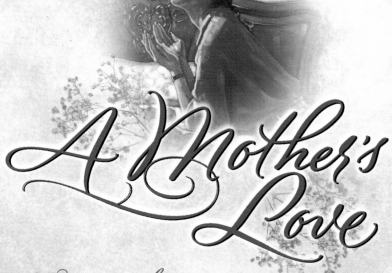

A Mother's Love

A Treasury of Honor & Inspiration

Based on the painting by

RON DiCIANNI

Compiled by

CAESAR KALINOWSKI

BROADMAN
& HOLMAN
PUBLISHERS

A Mother's Love is based on the painting by Ron DiCianni, text compiled by Caesar Kalinowski
Copyright © 2000 by Art2See, Inc. & Ron DiCianni
All rights reserved
Printed in China

0-8054-2370-2

Published by Broadman & Holman Publishers, Nashville, Tennessee
Design and Typesetting by Mozdren & Associates, St. Charles, Illinois

Library of Congress Catalog Card Number: 99-97262

1 2 3 4 5 04 03 02 01 00

Introduction

When wanting to describe how God will care for us He said, "As a mother comforts her child, so I will comfort you; and you will be comforted." Imagine God comparing His love by using the analogy of a mother!

There could be no greater compliment in the life of any who get the privilege to be called "Mom," than to hear God choose to use you as an example of His tenderness.

Many a hardened person has softened when reflecting on the comforting words that were tenderly spoken to them by a loving mother. The remembrance of her touch when the world scraped our knees, and later wounded our hearts, can bring most of us to tears.

The most vivid image I have of my mom is in prayer. I remember passing by her door and hearing her call out my name to God. Mom was the warrior on her knees for me, even when I didn't realize I needed one.

I will be forever grateful to God for my mother's love.

Ron DiCianni

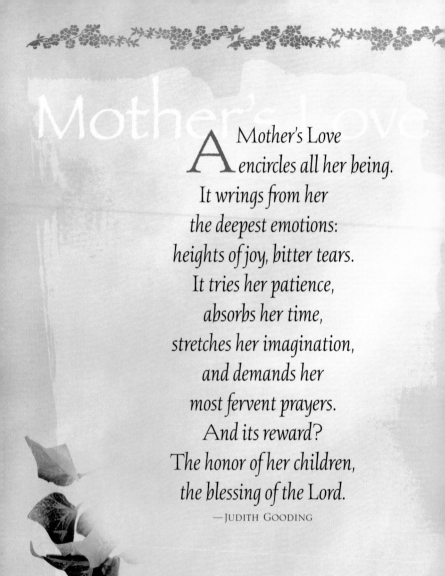

A Mother's Love
encircles all her being.
It wrings from her
the deepest emotions:
heights of joy, bitter tears.
It tries her patience,
absorbs her time,
stretches her imagination,
and demands her
most fervent prayers.
And its reward?
The honor of her children,
the blessing of the Lord.

—JUDITH GOODING

Most of all the other beautiful things in life
come by twos and threes,
by dozens and hundreds.
Plenty of roses, stars,
sunsets, rainbows,
brothers and sisters,
aunts and cousins,
but only one mother
in the whole world.

— KATE DOUGLAS WIGGIN

Who ran to help me when I fell
and would some pretty story tell,
or kiss the place to make it well?
My mother.

— ANN TAYLOR

The sweetest sounds
to mortals given
Are heard in Mother, Home,
and Heaven.

— WILLIAM GOLDSMITH BROWN

Youth fades, love droops,
The leaves of friendship fall;
A mother's secret hope
Outlives them all.

—OLIVER WENDELL HOLMES

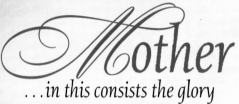

Mother
...in this consists the glory
and the most precious ornament of woman.

—LUTHER

Of all the friends we have,
our mother is the most loyal, the most steadfast.
Her love knows no limits.

—RHONDA S. HOGAN

To become a mother is not hard. To be a mother is.

—RHONDA S. HOGAN

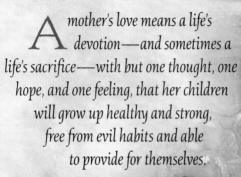

A mother's love means a life's
devotion—and sometimes a
life's sacrifice—with but one thought, one
hope, and one feeling, that her children
will grow up healthy and strong,
free from evil habits and able
to provide for themselves.

—AUTHOR UNKNOWN

As a mother comforts
her child, so I will
comfort you.

—ISAIAH 66:13 NIV

The ideal mother, like the ideal
marriage, is a fiction.

—MILTON R. SAPIRSTEIN

All mothers are rich when they love their children.
There are no poor mothers,
no ugly ones, no old ones.
Their love is always the most beautiful of the joys.

—MAURICE MAETERLINCK

A mother's love perceives
no impossibilities.

—PADDOCK

There is in all this world
no fount of deep, strong, deathless love,
save that within a mother's heart

—FELICIA HEMANS

Love never gives up,
never loses faith, is always hopeful, and endures
through every circumstance.

—I CORINTHIANS 13:7 NLT

Best Friend

A mother's love is indeed the golden link that binds youth to age; and he is still but a child, however time may have furrowed his cheek, or silvered his brow, who can yet recall, with a softened heart, the fond devotion, or the gentle chidings, of the best friend that God ever gives us.

—CHRISTIAN NESTELL BOVEE

Mother holds her children's hands for a while, their hearts forever.

—ANONYMOUS

The Haven of a Mother's Love

Her love is like an island
In life's ocean, vast and wide,
A peaceful, quiet shelter
From the wind, and rain, and tide.

Tis bound on the north by Hope,
By Patience on the west,
By tender Counsel on the south,
And on the east by Rest.

Above it like a beacon light
Shine faith, and truth, and prayer;
And through the changing scenes
Of life, I find a haven there.

—AUTHOR UNKNOWN

You are the light of the world…
Let your light shine before men in such a way
that they may see your good works and glorify
your Father who is in heaven.

—MATTHEW 5:14, 16 NASB

Kindness that portrays
A love that will endure,
Kindness that reveals
A hope that's strong and sure.
Kindness that remembers
A child along the way.

—ELIZABETH E. S. WILLIAMS

Encourage one another and build each other up,
just as in fact you are doing…
Always try to be kind to each other and to everyone else.

—1 THESSALONIANS 5:11, 15 NIV

L ove is patient and kind.
Love is not jealous or boastful or proud or rude.
Love does not demand its own way.
Love is not irritable, and it keeps no record
of when it has been wronged.
It is never glad about injustice but rejoices
whenever the truth wins out. Love never gives up,
never loses faith, is always hopeful,
and endures through
every circumstance.

—1 CORINTHIANS 13:4—7 NLT

*L*ove Is . . .

. . . *pacing the floor through the hours after
midnight, soothing your crying with
love-words and lullabies, when all of
my being is begging for rest.
Love is reading the same story over and over
and not taking any of it out.
Love is caring enough to say "no,"
even if "everybody else is doing it."
Love is letting you go with a lump in my throat,
a prayer in my heart, and a smile on my face, as
you stride out of the door to take on the world.*

—MARION STROUD

15

Love is not love
That alters when it alteration finds
Or bends with the remover to remove:
Oh no! It is an ever fixed mark
That looks on tempests and is never shaken.

—William Shakespeare

The love of a mother is never exhausted. It never
changes—it never tires—it endures through all, in good
repute, in bad repute, in the face of the world's condemnation,
a mother's love still lives on.

—Washington Irving

Dear children, let us not love
with words or tongue but
with actions and
in truth.

—1 John 3:18

NIV

Just One Touch

Everybody knows that a good mother gives her children a feeling of trust and stability. She is their earth. She is the one they can count on for the things that matter most of all. She is their food and their bed and the extra blanket when it grows cold in the night; she is their warmth and their health and their shelter; she is the one they want to be near when they cry. She is the only person in the whole world or in a whole lifetime who can be these things to her children. There is no substitute for her. Somehow even her clothes feel different to her children's hands from anybody else's clothes. Only to touch her skirt or her sleeve makes a troubled child feel better.

—KATHERINE BUTLER HATHAWAY

Let parents bequeath to their children not riches,
but the spirit of reverence.

—PLATO

Happy the son whose faith
in his mother remains unchanged.

—ALCOTT

No nation ever had a better friend
than the mother who taught
her children to pray.

—ANONYMOUS

There is no higher height to which
humanity can attain than that occupied
by a devoted, heaven-inspired, praying mother.

—ANONYMOUS

I prayed for this child and the LORD
has granted me what I asked of Him.

—1 Samuel 1:27 NIV

When I pray, my love as a mother meets
Your love as the Father. I call, and,
as You answer, the problems become promises,
the insecurities become wisdom, the fears
become faith. You always keep Your word:
You faithfully meet each need.

—Judith Gooding

God regards with how
much love a person
performs a work, rather
than how much he does.

—Thomas à Kempis

It's okay to open your heart, even if it must bleed a little. It's strength to admit when you're wrong and to apologize. It's strength to recognize how much you are able to love, beyond what you thought possible. On the other hand, it takes strength to recognize personal boundaries and pull them around you like a warm blanket. By allowing vulnerable experiences in quiet and rest, you become a person who makes every context a safe place. Your life becomes a shelter— whether giving a good night kiss to a child or listening to the secret dreams of a spouse. It starts every day at home.

—INGRID TROBISCH

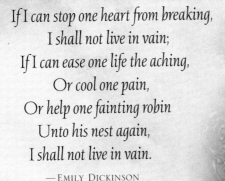

If I can stop one heart from breaking,
I shall not live in vain;
If I can ease one life the aching,
Or cool one pain,
Or help one fainting robin
Unto his nest again,
I shall not live in vain.

— EMILY DICKINSON

Maternal Love...
a miraculous substance which God
multiplies as He divides it.

— VICTOR HUGO

If anyone gives even a cup of cold water to one of these
little ones because he is my disciple, I tell you the truth,
he will certainly not lose his reward.

— MATTHEW 10:42 NIV

A definition I once heard of a mother is
"someone who hopes for you."

—FRANCIS GAY

A mother has a built-in worry mechanism...
without an off switch.

—PAM BROWN

The family is the only institution in the world where the
Kingdom of God can actually begin.

—ELTON TRUEBLOOD

At work, you think of the children you have left at home.
At home, you think of the work you've left unfinished.
Such a struggle is unleashed within yourself.
Your heart is rent.

—GOLDA MEIR

A rich child often sits in a poor mother's lap.

—DANISH PROVERB

All the World...

There is an enduring tenderness in the love of a mother to a son that transcends all other affections of the heart! It is neither to be chilled by selfishness, nor daunted by danger, nor weakened by worthlessness, nor stifled by ingratitude. She will sacrifice every comfort to his convenience; she will surrender every pleasure to his enjoyment; she will glory in his fame and exult in his prosperity — and if misfortune overtake him he will be the dearer to her from misfortune; and if disgrace settle upon his name she will still love and cherish him in spite of his disgrace; and if all the world beside cast him off she will be all the world to him.

— WASHINGTON IRVING

A Mother's Prayer

Lord, give me patience when wee hands
Tug at me with their small demands
Give me gentle and smiling eyes;
Keep my lips from hasty replies;
Let not weariness, confusion, or noise
Obscure my vision of life's fleeting joys.
So, when in years to come, my house is still—
No bitter memories its rooms may fill.

—AUTHOR UNKNOWN

Don't make your children angry by the way you treat
them. Rather, bring them up with the discipline
and instruction approved by the Lord.

—EPHESIANS 6:4 NLT

When home is ruled according to God's Word, angels might be asked to stay with us, and they would not find themselves out of their element.

—CHARLES H. SPURGEON

It is better to bind your children to you by a feeling of respect and by gentleness, than by fear.

—TERENCE

My son, hear the instruction of thy father, and forsake not the law of thy mother.

—PROVERBS 1:8 KJV

Praise your children openly, reprehend them secretly.

—W. CECIL

A Mother's Creed

I believe in the eternal importance of the home as the fundamental institution of society. I believe in the immeasurable possibilities of every boy and girl. I believe in the imagination, the trust, the hopes and the ideals which dwell in the hearts of all children. I believe in the beauty of nature, of art, of books, and of friendship. I believe in the satisfactions of duty. I believe in the little homely joys of everyday life. I believe in the goodness of the great design which lies behind our complex world. I believe in the safety and peace which surround us all through the overbrooding love of God.

—Ozora Davis

When you were small and just a touch away,
I covered you with blankets against the cool night air.
But now that you are tall and out of reach,
I fold my hands and cover you in prayer.

—AUTHOR UNKNOWN

His Mother

Even He that died for us upon the cross, in the last hour,
in the unutterable agony of death, was mindful of
His mother, as if to teach us that this holy love
should be our last worldly thought—
the last point of Earth from
which the soul should take
its flight for heaven. .

—HENRY WADSWORTH
LONGFELLOW

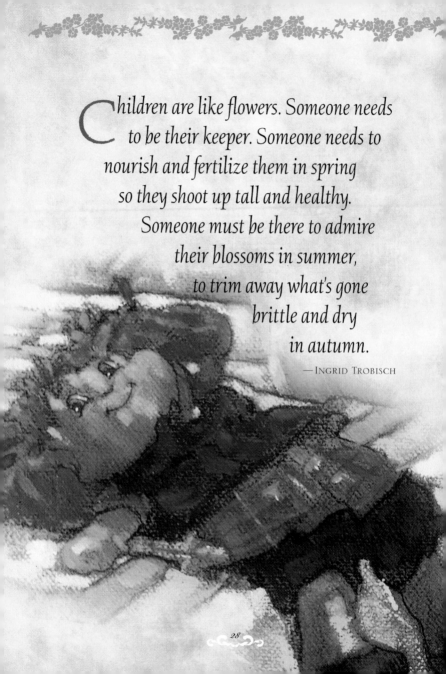

Children are like flowers. Someone needs
to be their keeper. Someone needs to
nourish and fertilize them in spring
so they shoot up tall and healthy.
Someone must be there to admire
their blossoms in summer,
to trim away what's gone
brittle and dry
in autumn.

—INGRID TROBISCH

The pain and pleasures of motherhood —
the worry and the joy —
are inexorably intertwined.
They come together, and we
simply must accept one with the
other. What we feel deep inside —
that powerful maternal bond —
is real and normal and part of God's
creative and procreative design.

— RUTH A. TUCKER

Be anxious for nothing, but in everything by prayer and
supplication with thanksgiving let your requests be made
known to God. And the peace of God, which surpasses
all comprehension, shall guard your hearts and your
minds in Christ Jesus.

— PHILIPPIANS 4:6 NASB

In the eyes of its mother, every beetle is a gazelle.

— MOROCCAN PROVERB

Some are kissing mothers and some are scolding mothers,
but it is love just the same, and most mothers
kiss and scold together.

—PEARL S. BUCK

My mother had a great deal of trouble with me,
but I think she enjoyed it.

—MARK TWAIN

"Isn't there one child you really love best?" a mother was
asked. And she replied, "Yes. The one who is sick, until he
gets well; the one who's away, until he gets home."

—ANONYMOUS

The mother-child relationship is paradoxical and,
in a sense, tragic. It requires the most intense love
on the mother's side, yet this very love must
help the child grow away from the mother,
and to become fully independent.

—ERICH FROMM

If a child lives with criticism
He learns to condemn;
If a child lives with hostility
He learns to fight;
If a child lives with ridicule
He learns to be shy;
If a child lives with shame
He learns to feel guilty.
But…
If a child lives with tolerance
He learns to be patient;
If a child lives with encouragement
He learns confidence;
If a child lives with praise
He learns to appreciate;
If a child lives with fairness
He learns justice;
If a child lives with security
He learns to have faith;
If a child lives with approval
He learns to like himself;
If a child lives with acceptance and friendship
He learns to find LOVE in the world!

—Dorothy Lawe Holt

A mother is a person who, seeing there are only
four pieces of pie for five people, promptly announces
she never did care for pie.

—TENNEVA JORDAN

I love little children, and it is not a slight thing when they,
who are fresh from God, love us.

—CHARLES DICKENS

These are the children God has graciously given to me.

—GENESIS 33:5 NLT

Our children are likely to live up
to what we believe of them.

—LADY BIRD JOHNSON

A Mother's Love...

Can look beyond
the problem to a promise,

It can build
a holy temple
from a formless pile of clay.

And when the chance
of victory's waning,
Love keeps on believing,

And it searches out
God's heart for wisdom
as it kneels to pray.

—JUDITH GOODING

She is clothed with strength and dignity;
she can laugh at the days to come. Her
children arise and call her blessed; her husband
also, and he praises her: "Many women do
noble things, but you surpass them all."

—PROVERBS 31:25, 28 — 29 KJV

A mother's children are portraits of herself.

—UNKNOWN

The mother's heart is the child's schoolroom.

—HENRY WARD BEECHER

Who takes the child by the hand
takes the mother by the heart.

—DANISH PROVERB

Not until I became a mother did I understand
    How much my mother had sacrificed for me.
Not until I became a mother did I feel
    How hurt my mother was when I disobeyed.
Not until I became a mother did I know
    How proud my mother was when I achieved.
Not until I became a mother did I realize
    How much my mother loves me.
        —Therefore, be encouraged.
One day, your children will feel the same way.

—VICTORIA FARNSWORTH

The Watcher

She always leaned to watch for us,
Anxious if we were late,
In winter by the window,
In summer by the gate;

And though we mocked
her tenderly,
Who had such foolish care,
The long way home would
seem more safe
Because she waited there.

Her thoughts were all so full of us,
She never could forget!
And so I think that where she is
She must be watching yet,

Waiting til we come home to her,
Anxious if we are late —
Watching from Heaven's window,
Leaning from Heaven's gate.

— MARGARET WIDDEMER

When God thought of mother,
He must have laughed with satisfaction,
and framed it quickly—
so rich, so deep, so divine,
so full of soul, power, and beauty,
was the conception.

—HENRY WARD BEECHER

People who say they sleep like
a baby usually don't have one.

—LEO J. BURKE

Behold, children are a gift of the LORD;
The fruit of the womb is a reward.

—PSALM 127:3 NASB

Children can have no better inheritance than believing
parents. Religion can become real in the midst of the
family as in practically no other way. Many of us have
inherited great riches from our parents—the bank
account of their personal faith and family prayers.

—NELS F.S. FERRE

The mother love is like God's love;
He loves us not because we are lovable,
but because it is His nature to love,
and because we are His children.

— EARL RINEY

Over my slumbers your loving watch keep;
Rock me to sleep, Mother; rock me to sleep.

— ELIZABETH AKERS ALLEN

The Bible does not say very much about homes;
it says a great deal about the things that make them.
It speaks about life and love and joy and peace and rest!
If we get a house and put these into it,
we shall have secured a home.

— JOHN HENRY JOWETT

A mother understands what a child does not say.

— JEWISH PROVERB

Memories

Like a richly colored flame whose bright tip
draws upward, but is brushed by erring
storm, then relentingly seeks the earth's dark
form and buries its deep desires bit by bit; thus
your life ebbed — through trembling, pleading
lips cried proffering words to a triune God.
In vain I watched for one familiar nod, then
pressed my mouth to thin black hairy wisps.
Memories? Mother! How can I forget?
Your smiling eyes with sad mystery tinged;
Your helping hands, though labor wrought
with tasks; Mother! Your clear high laughter
had a depth that thrilled my heart,
and lifted silence winged with boundless
joy. Thank God! Memories last!

—Hilda A. Dammirc

I found myself remembering that my mother's strongest belief was that all things happen for a reason. She would say we may not understand the why of such things, but if we accept them and go forward, we find, down the road a ways, there was a reason and that everything happens for the best. Her greatest gift to me was an abiding and unshakable faith in God.

—RONALD REAGAN

A Special Gift

There never was a woman like her. She was gentle as a dove and brave as a lioness. The memory of my mother and her teachings were, after all, the only capital I had to start life with, and on that capital I have made my way.

—ANDREW JACKSON

For when you looked into my mother's eyes you
knew, as if He had told you, why God sent her
into the world — it was to open the minds of
all who looked to beautiful thoughts.

—SIR JAMES M. BARRIE

My Mother

She was as good as goodness is. Her acts and
all her words were kind, and high above all
memories I hold the beauty of her mind.

—FREDERIC HENTZ ADAMS

Mothers have as powerful an influence
over the welfare of future generations
as all other earthly causes combined.

—JOHN S. C. ABBOT

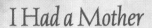

I Had a Mother

You may have tangible wealth untold;
Caskets of jewels and coffers of gold.
Richer than I, you can never be—
I had a mother who read to me.

—STRICKLAND GILLILAN

Stories first heard at mother's
knee are never wholly
forgotten — a little
spring that never
quite dries up in our
journey through
scorching years.

—G. RUFFINI

I remember my mother's prayers;
they have clung to me all my life.

—ABRAHAM LINCOLN

My mother was the most beautiful woman I ever saw. All I am I owe to my mother. I attribute all my success in life to the moral, intellectual, and physical education I received from her.

—George Washington

What would you take?

What would you take for that soft little head
Pressed close to your face at time for bed;
For the white, dimpled hand in your own held tight,
And the dear little eyelids kissed down for the night?

What would you take?

What would you take for that smile in the morn,
Those bright, dancing eyes and the face they adorn:
For the sweet little voice that you hear all day
Laughing and cooing — yet nothing to say?

What would you take?

What would you take for those pink little feet,
Those chubby round cheeks, and that mouth so sweet;
For the wee tiny fingers and little soft toes,
The wrinkly little neck and that funny little nose?
Now, what would you take?

—GOOD HOUSEKEEPING

My Mother

My mother was the making of me.
She was so true and so sure of me
I felt I had something to live for,
someone I must not disappoint.
The memory of my mother
will always be a blessing to me.

—THOMAS A. EDISON

Love at Home

There is beauty all around
When there's love at home;
There is joy in every sound
When there's love at home.

Peace and plenty here abide,
Smiling sweet on every side;
Time doth softly, sweetly glide
When there's love at home.

—AUTHOR UNKNOWN

Love and Pet Me Now

Take my withered hands in yours,
Children of my soul;
Mother's heart is craving love;
Mother's growing old.
See, the snows of many years
Crown my furrowed brow;
As I've loved and petted you,
Love and pet me now.
Take my withered hands in yours,
Hold them close and strong;
Cheer me with a fond caress,
Twill not be for long;
Youth immortal soon will crown
With its wreath my brow.
As I've loved and petted you,
Love and pet me now.

—T. B. LARIMORE